DESIGN AND CREATE

Things to Wear

Margot Richardson

RSVP

RAINTREE STECK-VAUGHN PUBLISHERS

The Steck-Vaughn Company

Austin, Texas

Published by Raintree Steck-Vaughn Publishers,
an imprint of Steck-Vaughn Company

Library of Congress Cataloging-in-Publication Data
Richardson, Margot.
Things to wear / Margot Richardson.
p. cm.—(Design and create)
Includes bibliographical references and index.
Summary: Lists required items and step-by-step instructions for making dress accesories such as a neck tie, hair clips, spectacles, slip-on shoes, face mask, friendship band, and necklace.
ISBN 0-8172-4888-9
1. Handicraft—Juvenile literature.
2. Dress accessories—Juvenile literature.
3. Paper work—Juvenile literature.
4. Children—Costume—Juvenile literature.
[1. Dress accessories. 2. Paper work. 3. Costume.
4. Handicraft.]
I. Title. II. Series: Williams, John, 1939- Design and create.
TT160.R44 1998
745.5—dc21 97-13923

Printed in Italy. Bound in the United States.
1 2 3 4 5 6 7 8 9 0 02 01 00 99 98

Commissioned photography by Zul Mukhida

CONTENTS

INTRODUCTION

An Aboriginal theater group from northern Australia performing a tribal dance. For special ceremonies, dancers decorate their bodies with paints made from colored earth.

Many thousands of years ago, people started to wear clothes to keep themselves warm. The first clothes were made of animal skins and furs.

About 5,000 years ago, people learned how to make fabric, or cloth. Fabric can be made in many different colors, and people began to make clothes in various shapes.

The types of clothes worn around the world depend a great deal on the climate. People who live in cold countries must wear heavy clothes to keep them warm. People in hot countries wear less so that they can stay cool.

Of course, we do not wear clothes just for warmth—we like to look attractive and to wear clothes in styles and colors that suit us. We also choose hairstyles and decorate our bodies with makeup and jewelry.

Early people dressed up with necklaces made of shells and seeds, and they even painted themselves with colors found in the earth. When metals and jewels were discovered, jewelry became colorful, shiny, and highly prized.

People wear different things at different times. Some clothes are worn almost every day. Others are kept for special occasions such as holidays.

Some of the things we put on our bodies, such as jewelry, are worn just to look interesting.

Other things do a particular job. For example, sunglasses screen our eyes from the sun, and scarves keep our necks warm.

People want the things they wear to look good. But designers have a special job to do. Besides making the clothes look attractive, they must make things work properly. A raincoat needs to be waterproof; a bathing suit should dry quickly; a pair of shoes must be hard-wearing and last for months or even years.

Things that are worn include clothes, shoes, jewelry, and makeup. We often decide what people are like from the way they look.

Think about the things you wear each day.

- Write a list of the things you are wearing now.
- What are they made of?
- What different things do you wear when you go somewhere special, for example, to a party?

Lapp people live in northern Norway, where there is often snow all year round. These traditional clothes were designed to keep out the cold.

ROYAL CROWN

YOU WILL NEED

- Gold or yellow poster board
- Large colored beads that look like jewels
- Fake fur (optional)
- Two adhesive Velcro pieces
- Large sheet of paper
- Tape measure
- Glue
- Pencil
- Ruler
- Scissors

For hundreds of years, the kings and queens of Europe have worn crowns on special occasions. A crown shows that the king or queen is the most important person in the country.

Here is a crown you can make out of simple materials. Use it for a school play or a history project.

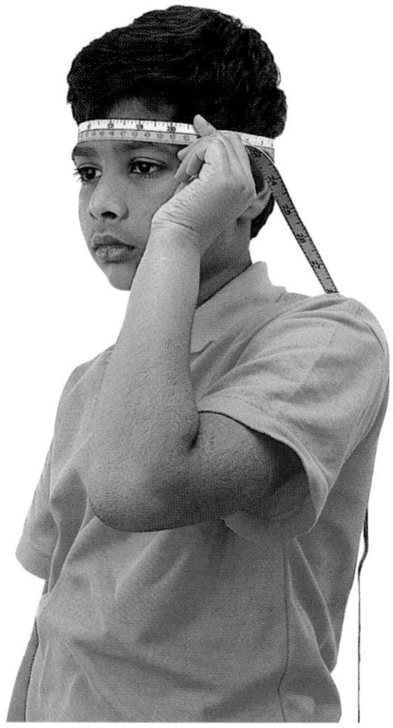

1 Decide how big the crown has to be. Measure around your head, just above the ears, with a tape measure. Add 2 in. (5 cm) to this length.

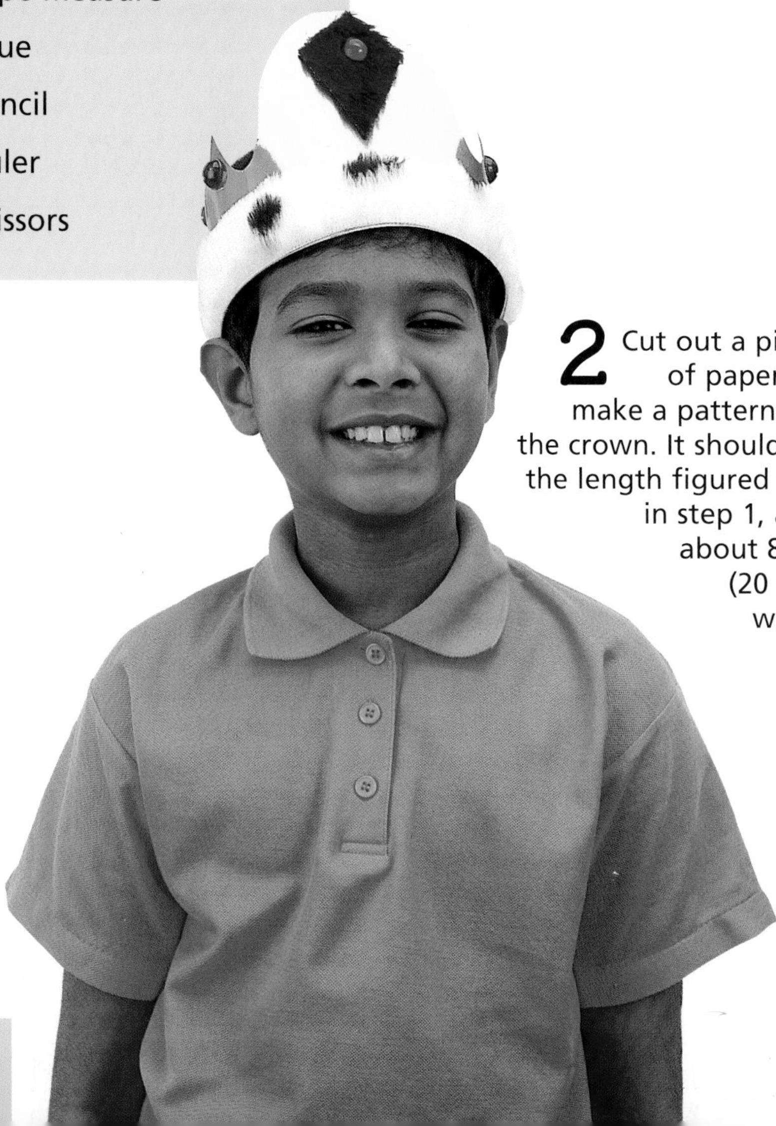

2 Cut out a piece of paper, to make a pattern for the crown. It should be the length figured out in step 1, and about 8 in. (20 cm) wide.

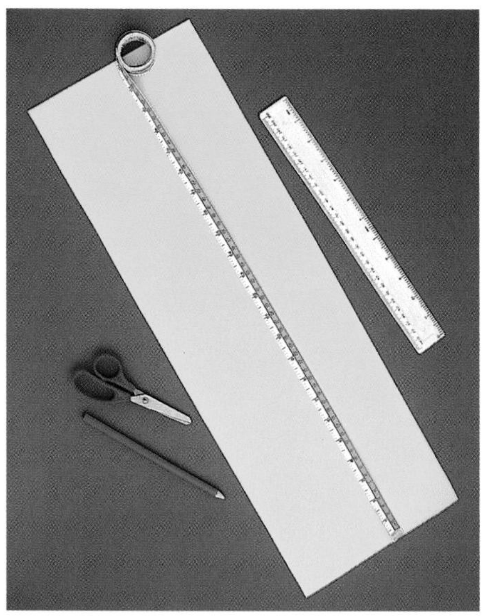

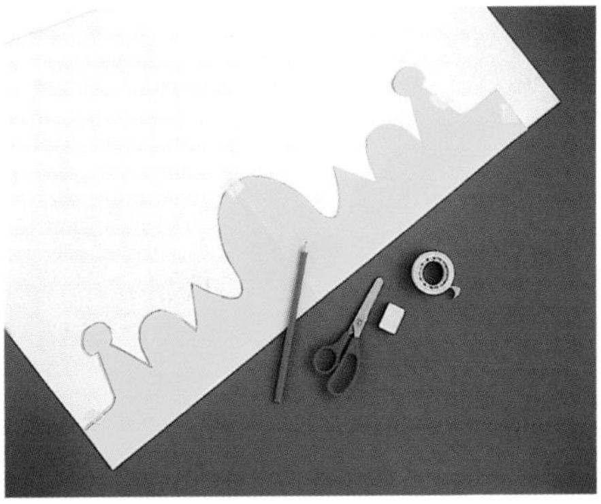

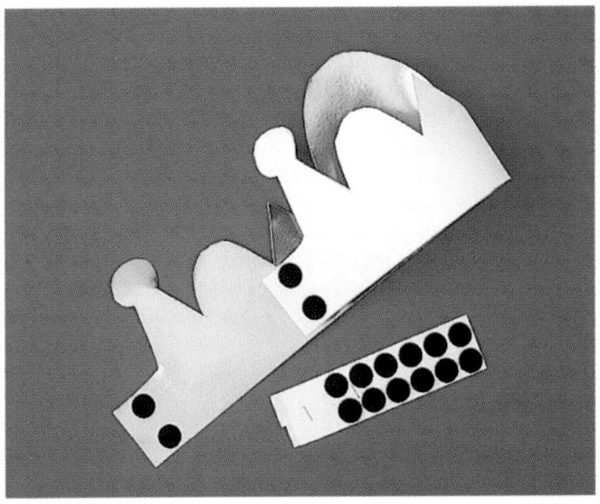

3 Fold the piece of paper in half. Draw the shape of the crown on one side of the paper. When you are happy with the shape, cut it out.

4 Unfold the paper pattern and put it on the plain side of the poster board. Draw around the shape. Cut the shape out of the poster board.

5 Put the Velcro pieces at either end of the crown, about .5 in. (1.5 cm) in from the edge. The hard pieces should go on the gold side. Stick the soft pieces on the plain side.

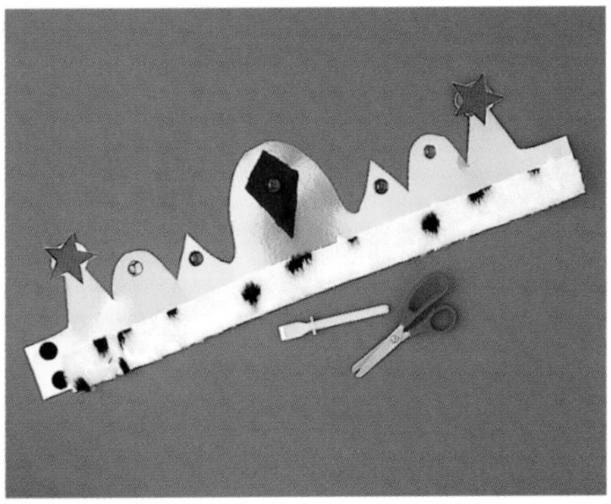

6 Decorate the crown. Glue on beads to look like jewels. You can also stick on fake fur along the bottom edge.

Queen Elizabeth II of England wears a crown on important days such as the State Opening of the British Parliament. This crown is made of gold, which is very heavy. It is decorated with some of the biggest gems in the world. The fur at the bottom makes it more comfortable to wear.

BOW TIE

YOU WILL NEED

- Scraps of fabric, preferably crisp cotton
- Dressmaking elastic, about .25 in. (1 cm) wide x 16 in. (40 cm) long
- 3 small safety pins
- Tape measure
- Pencil
- Ruler
- Scissors

Ties are worn mainly by men. They are called ties because they are tied around the neck with special knots. Here is a way of making a bow tie that is easy to put on.

Before you start, make sure the fabric does not have any creases in it. Ask an adult to iron it for you if necessary.

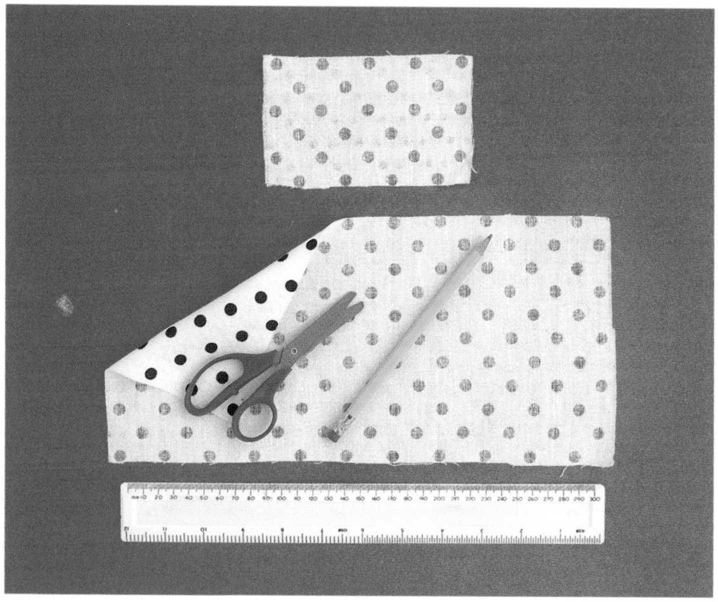

1 Draw two rectangles on the wrong side of the fabric. One piece should be about 13 x 6 in. (32 x 15 cm). The other should measure about 5 x 3 in. (13 x 7.5 cm). Cut the pieces out.

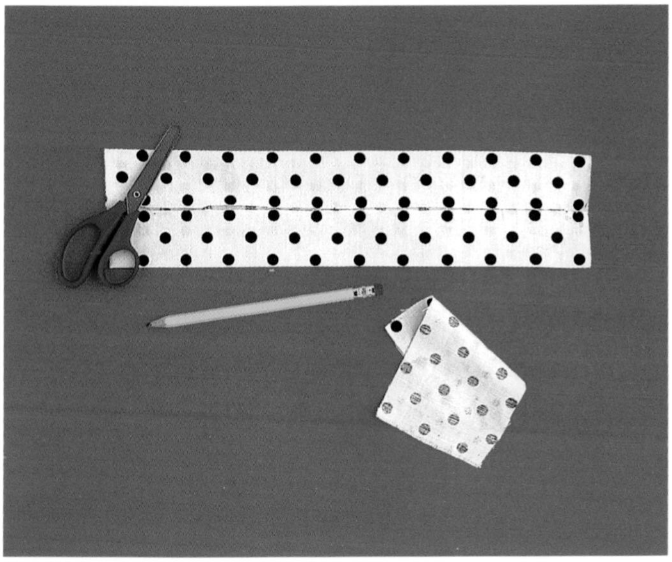

2 Fold the larger piece of fabric lengthwise, turning both the long edges into the center. Make creases along the folds by pressing them with your fingertips.

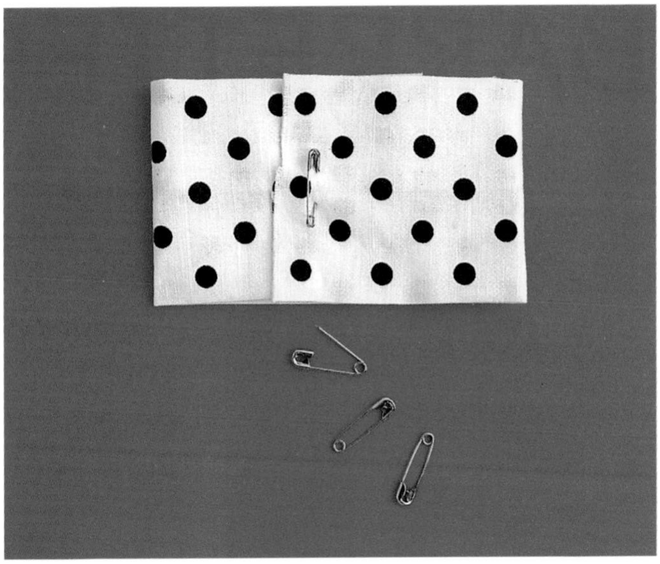

3 Fold this piece of fabric again but in the other direction, so that it overlaps at the back by about 2 in. (5 cm). Hold it in place with a safety pin.

4 Fold the smaller piece of fabric in the same way as in step 2. Then fold it around the larger piece at right angles, to make the bow shape. Use another safety pin to hold it.

5 Take the piece of elastic. Pin both ends to the back of the bow tie. Put the tie on to see if the elastic is too long or too short. Change the length of the elastic if necessary.

NOW TRY THIS

Make some more ties that are different shapes. Try a long thin necktie shape or a much bigger, floppier bow tie.

MAKE YOUR OWN HAT

Hats can be many different shapes and made out of all sorts of materials. Some hats are hard and others are soft.

Hats are worn for many reasons. In hot countries they are used to shade faces from the sun. They are also useful to keep our heads dry when it rains and to make sure they stay warm during a cold winter. Sometimes a hat can show how important someone is.

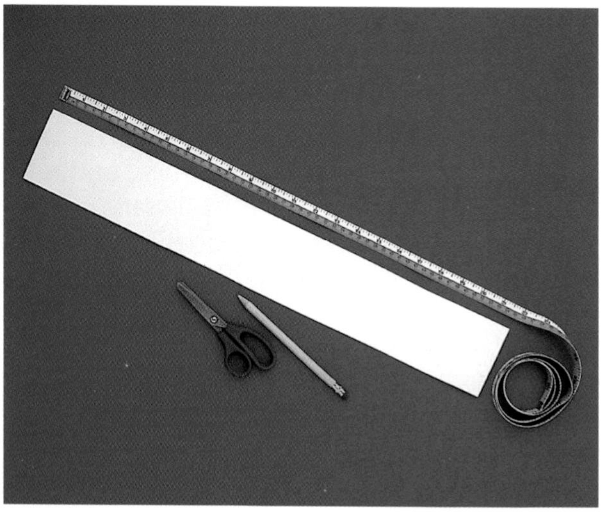

1 Measure around your head with the tape measure, just above the ears. On a piece of poster board, draw a long rectangle. It should be the length you measured, plus another 1 in. (2 cm), and about 3 in. (7.5 cm) wide.

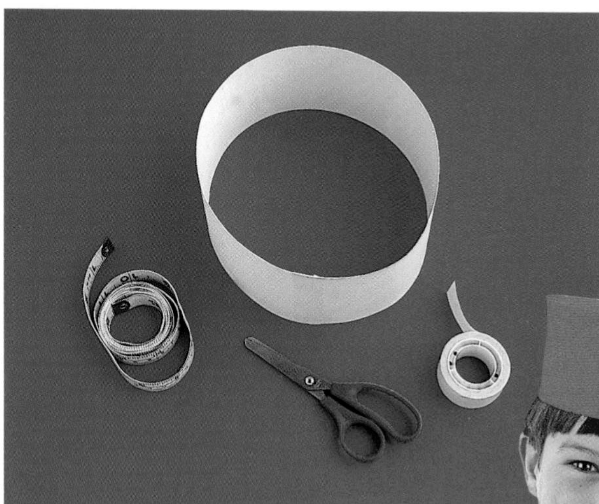

2 Cut out the rectangle. Bend it into a circle and join it lightly at the short ends with masking tape. The ends should overlap a little. Put the circle on your head to see if it fits.

YOU WILL NEED

- Large sheet of poster board
- Fabric or felt for covering
- Decoration such as yarn, ribbon, tassel, etc. (optional)
- Masking tape
- Glue
- Tape measure
- Pencil
- Ruler
- Scissors

3 Stand this circle on a piece of poster board. Draw around the circle, making sure not to push it out of shape. Cut out the flat disk. This will form a pattern for the top of the hat.

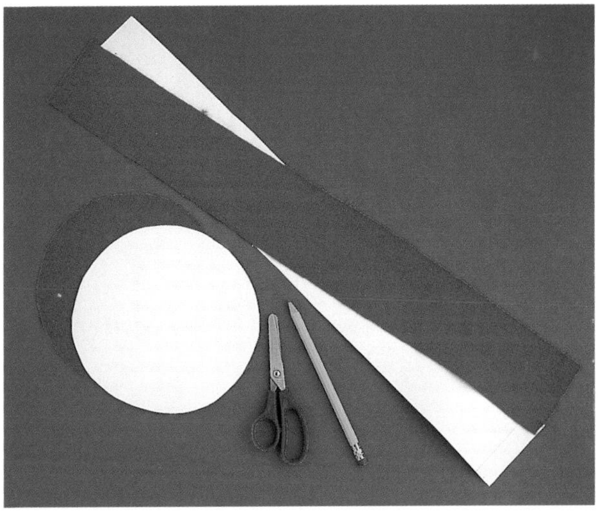

4 Undo the tape on the long piece of poster board. Use the two poster board pieces as patterns to draw the same two shapes on the fabric or felt. Then cut them out.

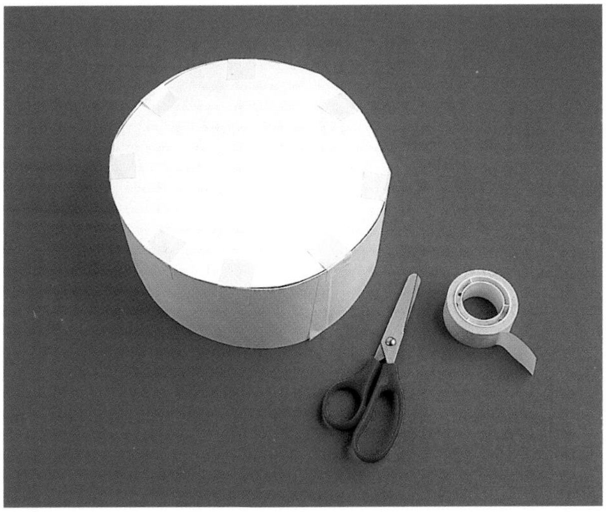

5 Make the hat shape, using the pieces of poster board. Rejoin the ends of the long piece, as in step 2. Then stick the top of the hat to the sides with small pieces of masking tape.

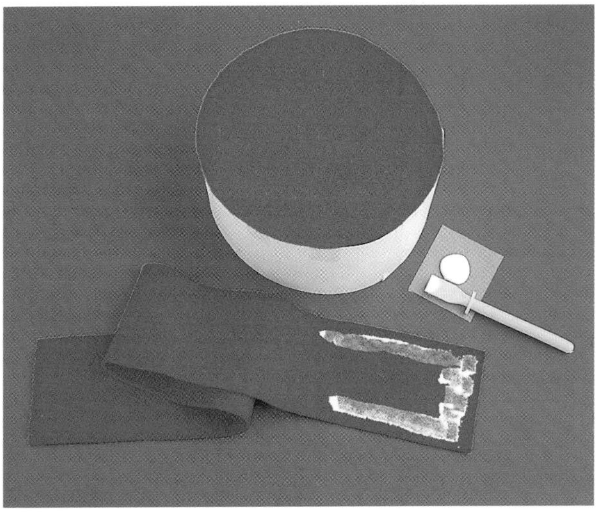

6 When the poster board shape is finished, glue the fabric pieces to it. Make sure there is no poster board showing. You may want to add decorations, such as a tassel on top or a colored band around the side.

NOW TRY THIS

Once you have made a basic hat, add a brim: put the finished hat on a large piece of poster board, draw around it carefully, then draw a larger circle around the first one. Cut out the poster board ring and tape it to the lower edge of the hat. Cover it with fabric, as in step 6.

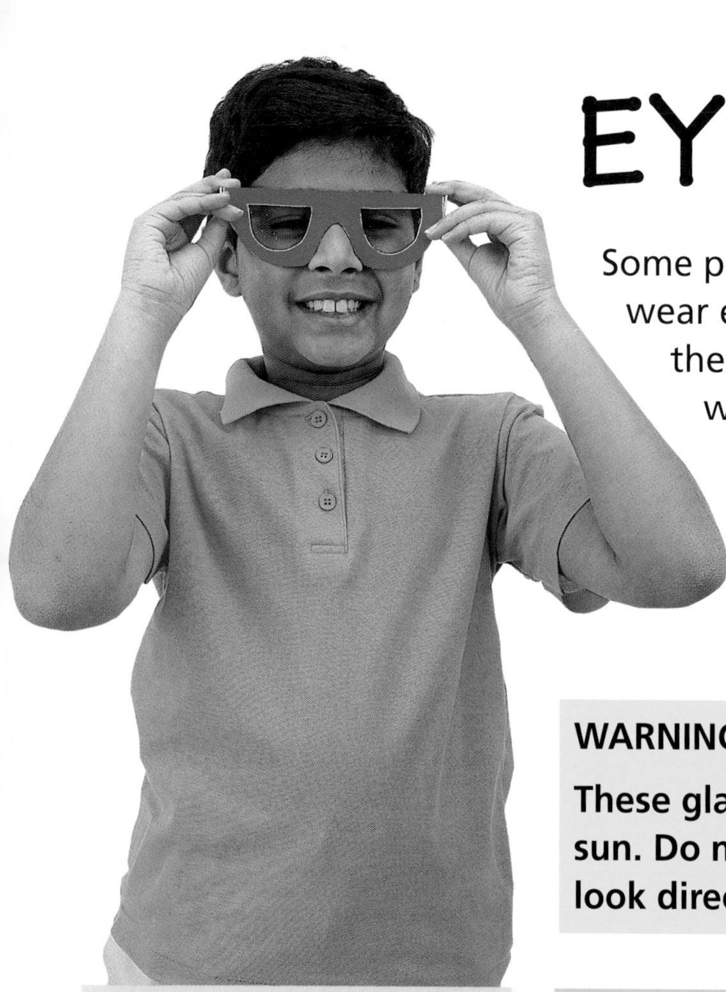

EYEGLASSES

Some people cannot see as well as others. They wear eyeglasses with special lenses to improve their eyesight. People also wear sunglasses, with colored lenses, to shade their eyes from bright sunlight.

The eyeglasses shown here do not work like real glasses, but show you a way of making a frame with hinges.

WARNING!

These glasses will not protect your eyes from the sun. Do not wear them for long periods, and *never* look directly at the sun.

YOU WILL NEED

- Two different types or colors of poster board
- Colored plastic or acetate sheets
- Plain paper
- Masking tape
- Pencil
- Ruler
- Scissors

1 Draw a rectangle on a piece of paper. It should be about 6 in. (15 cm) long, and 2 to 3 in. (5 to 7.5 cm) wide. Cut it out and fold it in half.

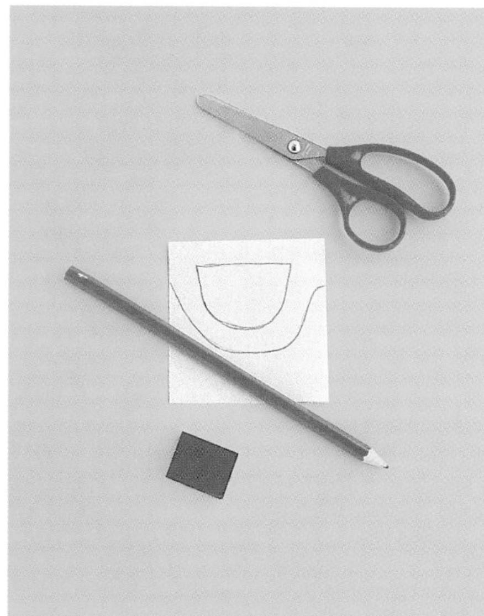

2 Draw the shape of one side of the eyeglasses on the paper. Put the space for the nose at the edge of the paper. Cut out the shape, through both thicknesses of the paper, to make a shape that is the same on either side.

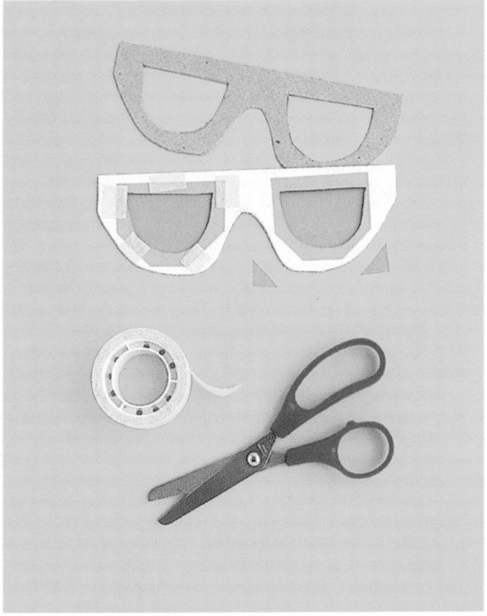

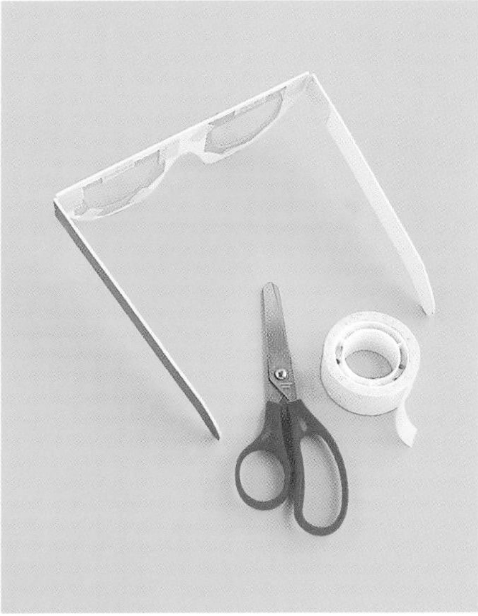

3 Use the paper pattern to draw the frame shape on two different colors of poster board. Also cut out two arms, again in the two colors. The arms must be mirror images of each other.

4 Cut pieces of colored plastic or acetate to make the "lenses." They should be slightly larger than the holes to be covered. Stick them onto the wrong side of the poster board with small pieces of masking tape.

5 Join the arms to the frames with pieces of masking tape, to make hinges. Make sure the hinges can bend freely.

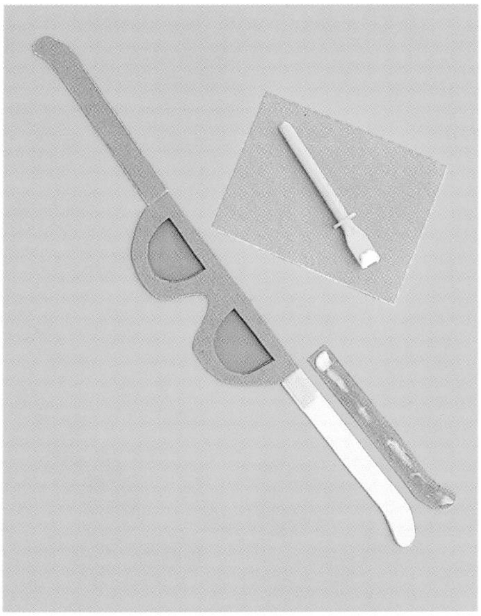

6 Glue the two frames to each other, with their wrong sides together. The plastic lenses should be sandwiched in the middle of the finished frame.

Sunglasses have dark lenses to shade eyes from the sun. Although the name makes them sound as though they are made of glass, many eyeglasses are now made of plastic.

NOW TRY THIS

Now that you have made some basic eyeglasses, design some shapes that are more interesting. They could be square, round, or oval. Decorate the front of the frame with paints or glue on glitter or beads.

SANDALS

YOU WILL NEED

- Thick corrugated cardboard, from a carton or box
- Colored paper or fabric
- Poster board
- Self-adhesive vinyl
- Glue
- Masking tape
- Tape measure
- Pencil
- Scissors

Shoes protect our feet. They let us walk over rough ground without hurting our feet, and they keep our feet warm when it is cold.

But shoes can do all sorts of other jobs, too. Think of the difference between slippers worn by a ballerina and the boots worn by a worker on a building site. Some shoes can be very plain, whereas others are brightly colored and decorated.

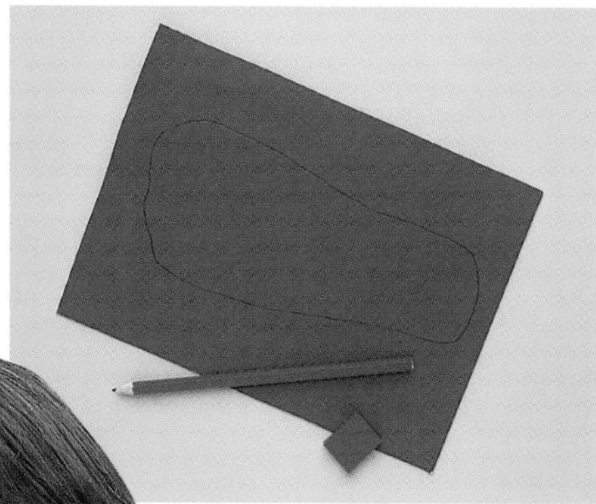

1 Put your foot on a piece of poster board and draw around it with a pencil. Do the same for the other foot. Then cut out the foot shapes.

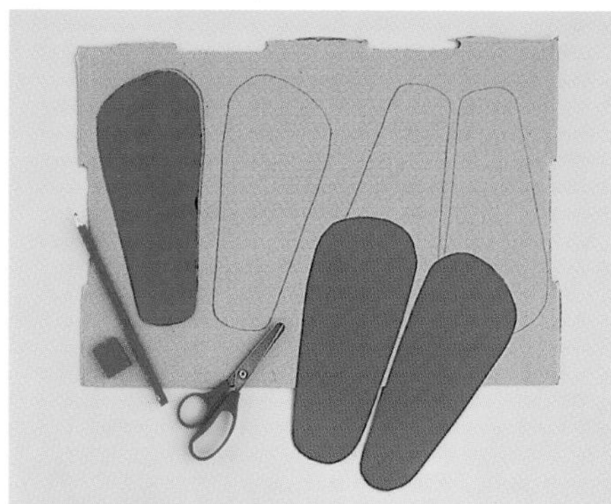

2 Put the foot patterns on the thick cardboard and mark out two pieces for each foot. Mark them Left and Right and cut them out. Cut another left and right shape from colored paper or fabric.

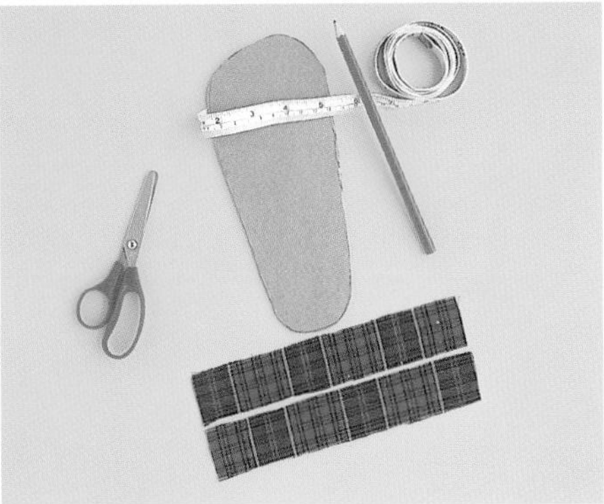

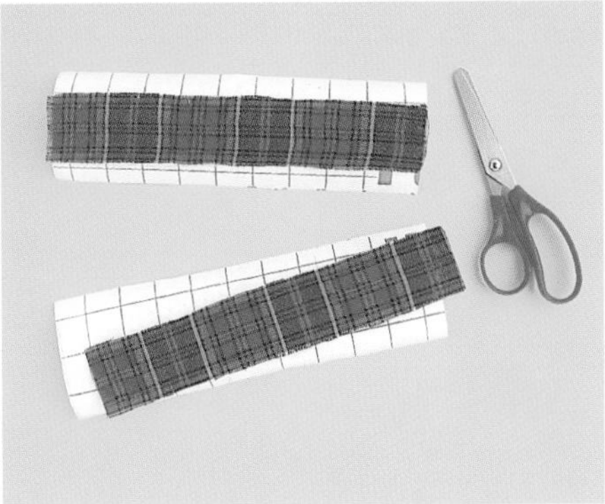

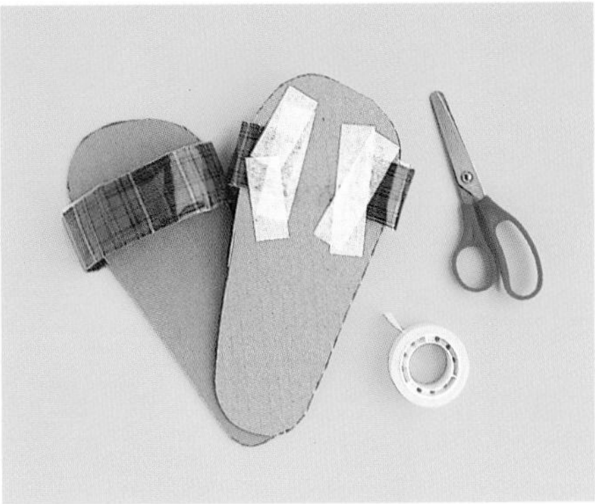

3 Measure around the widest part of your foot with a tape measure; add 2 in. (5 cm). Cut out two pieces of colored paper or fabric. They should be the length above, and about 1.5 in. (4 cm) wide.

4 Cut two pieces of adhesive vinyl, the same length as in step 3, but much wider. Peel off the paper backing and put the colored paper or fabric in the center of the sticky side of the vinyl. Fold over the edges of the vinyl and stick them down.

5 Put one of the vinyl-covered strips over the widest part of a cardboard "foot." It should overlap each side by about 1 in. (2.5 cm). Stick it in place underneath with the masking tape.

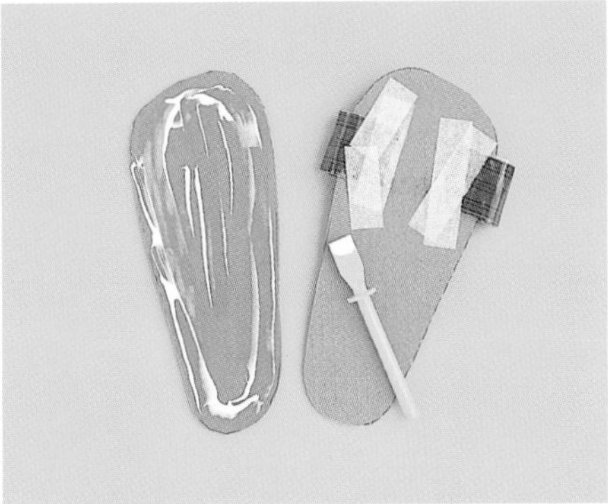

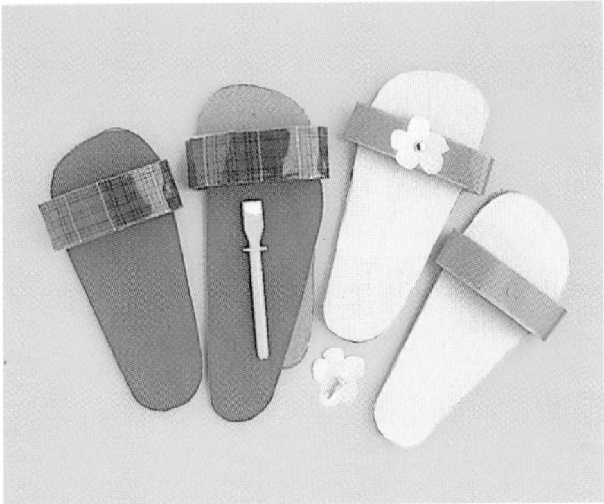

6 Glue the matching cardboard shape to the underside of the shoe. Make sure the ends of the vinyl-covered strip are stuck neatly between the two layers.

7 Glue the colored foot shape to the top surface of the shoe. If you wish, add some extra decoration to the top of the shoe.

Shoes are most often made in factories, but this shoemaker in Pakistan makes and sells shoes in a small shop.

NOW TRY THIS

Design another pair of shoes, with a different shape that covers the foot. You could add a strap to go around the back of your heel. Experiment to find the best way of attaching this to the piece at the front.

FACE MASK

YOU WILL NEED

- Poster board
- Plain paper
- Scraps of colored paper, egg cartons, fabric, etc., for shapes and decoration
- Elastic, about .25 in. (5 mm) wide and 12 in. (30 cm) long
- Two metal paper fasteners
- Glue
- Masking tape
- Pencil
- Ruler
- Scissors
- Paints (optional)

A mask is a covering that hides a person's face. Masks have been worn by different people around the world for many thousands of years.

Some masks are for safety, such as masks worn by doctors or by catchers in baseball. Others are worn at parties or festivals, by actors in the theater, or for special ceremonies.

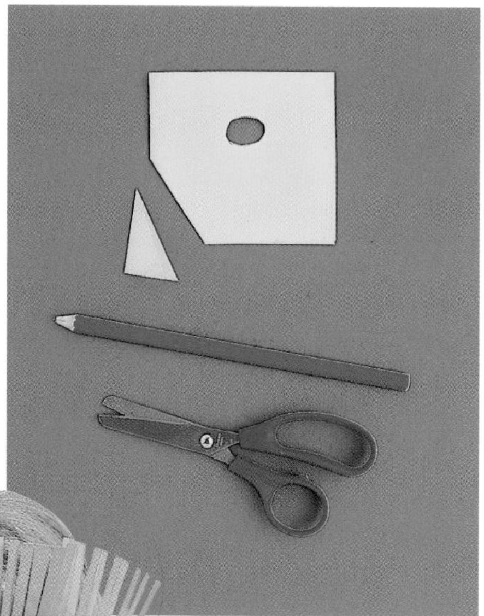

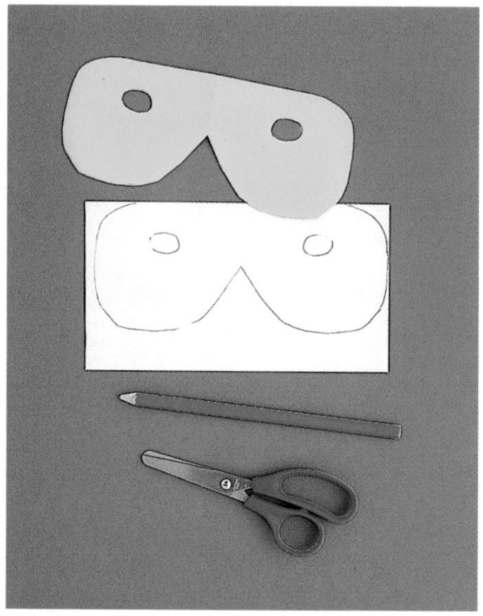

1 Cut a rectangle of paper, about 7 in. x 3 in. (18 x 8 cm). Fold it in half and cut an upside-down V in the center. Also cut holes to see through.

2 Try the paper over your face to see if it fits. Change the shape if necessary. Use it as a pattern and cut the shape out of poster board.

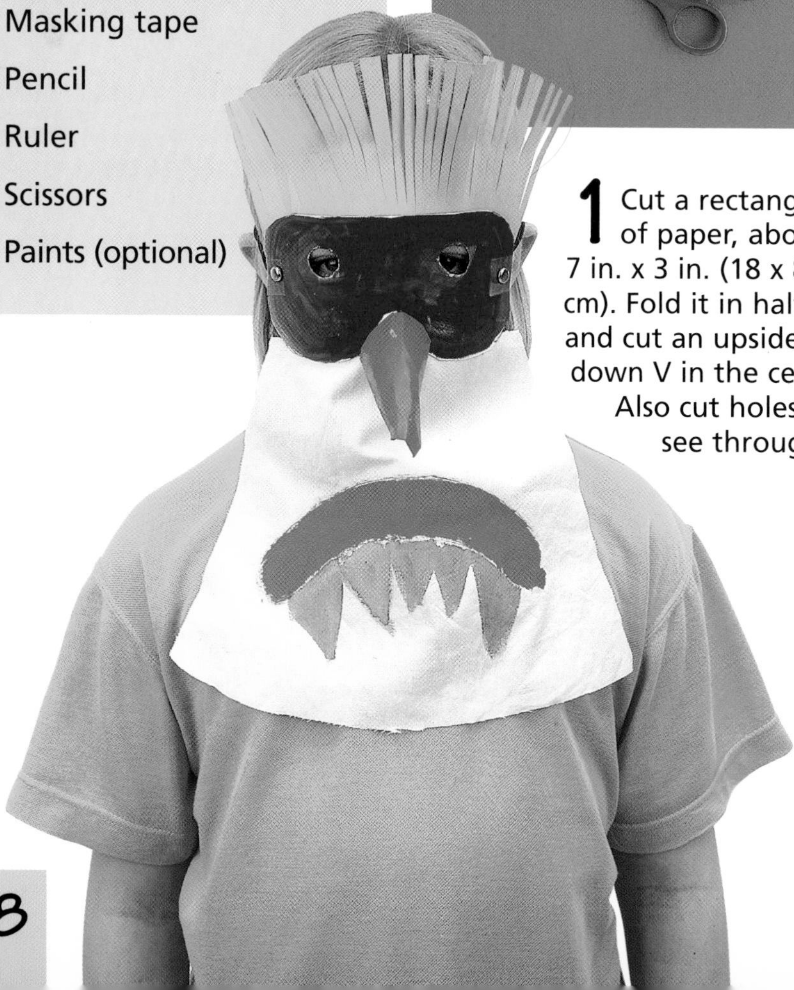

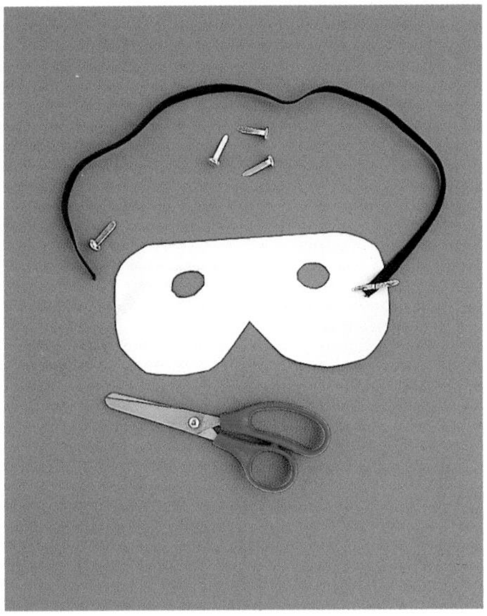

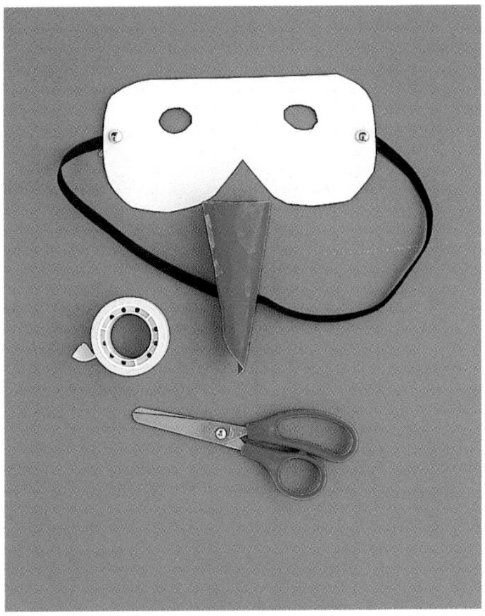

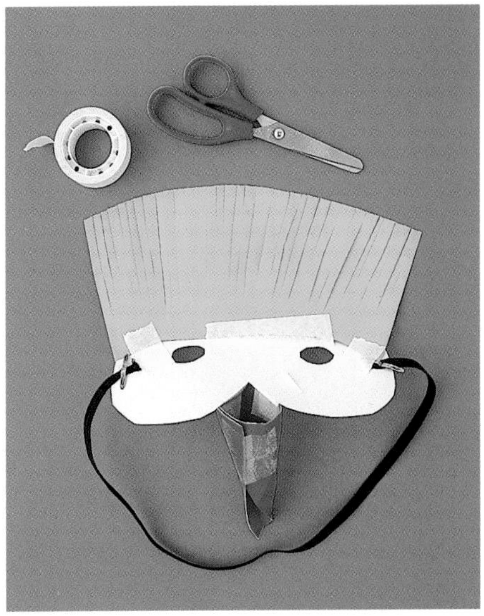

3 Fasten the elastic on one side with a paper fastener. Hold the mask on your face and figure out how much elastic is needed around the back of your head to hold the mask on firmly. Join the elastic to the other side with another paper fastener.

4 Add a nose to the mask. It could be made from part of an egg carton or a piece of rolled or folded poster board. Stick it on with masking tape. Check that the nosepiece fits over your nose.

5 Add something to the top of the mask to hide your hair. It could be made of paper or fabric. Tape or glue it to the top of the eye covering.

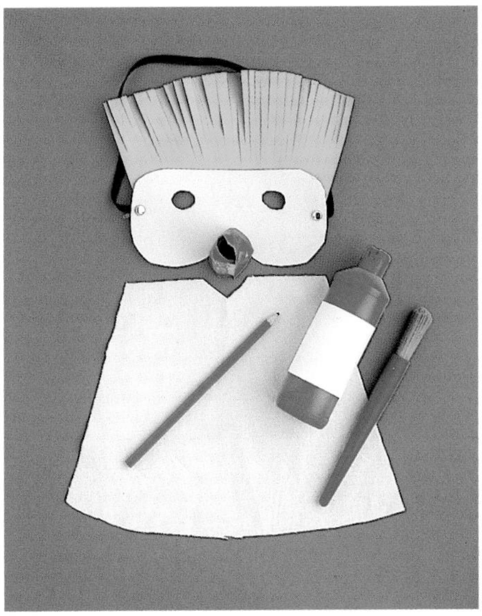

6 You may wish to add a lower piece to the mask to cover the rest of your face. Use your imagination to make it look as different as possible from the way your face normally looks.

A large mask can completely change the way you look, making you look like an animal or a monster. This mask comes from Matabeleland, in Zimbabwe.

NECKLACE

YOU WILL NEED

- Colored wrapping paper
- Short piece of wooden dowel, about .25 in. (5 mm) in diameter
- Colored embroidery floss
- Colored beads (optional)
- Petroleum jelly
- Glue
- Pencil & ruler
- Scissors
- Darning needle

A necklace is a kind of jewelry. Necklaces can be made out of many things, from leaves and flowers to precious gems such as diamonds.

Here is a way of making your own necklace, with beads made out of nothing more than a piece of colored paper.

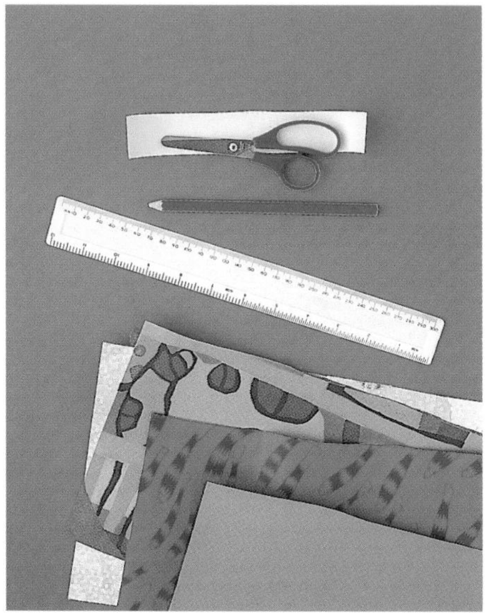

1 Decide on the length of your necklace. Put a piece of the floss around a friend's neck and figure out what length looks best. Take the thread off, add about 1 in. (2.5 cm) (to allow for a knot) and cut it.

2 Decide on the width of the beads. They can be anything from about .25 in. to 1.5 in. (1 cm to 4 cm). Turn the paper over so that it is plain side up. Measure out a long strip, .5 to 1.5 in. (1 to 4 cm) wide, and at least 8 in. (20 cm) long.

In some countries jewelry is worn just by women, but in others, both men and women decorate their bodies in this way. These dancers from Tokelau, tiny islands in the middle of the Pacific Ocean, wear shell necklaces.

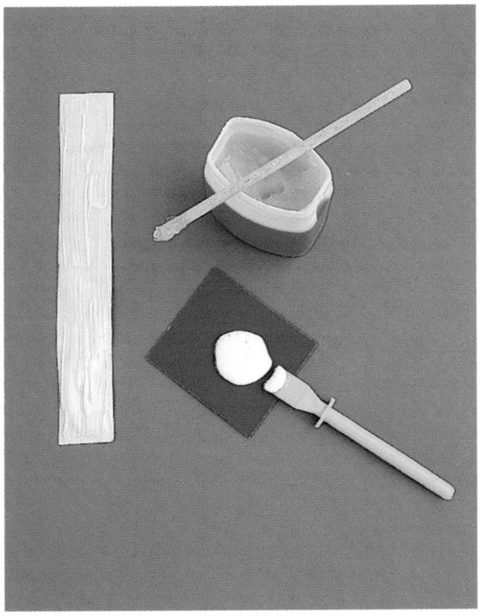

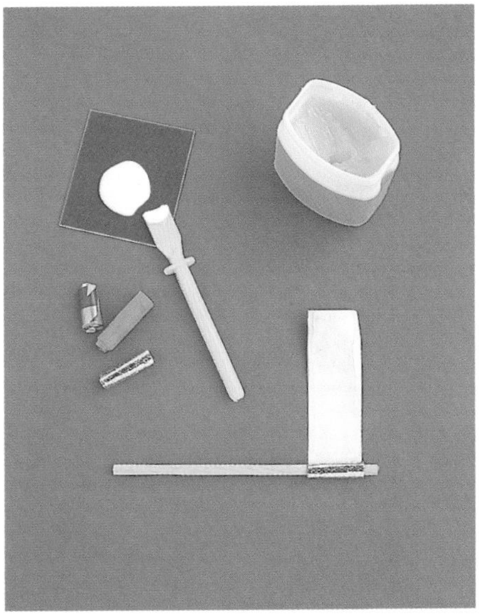

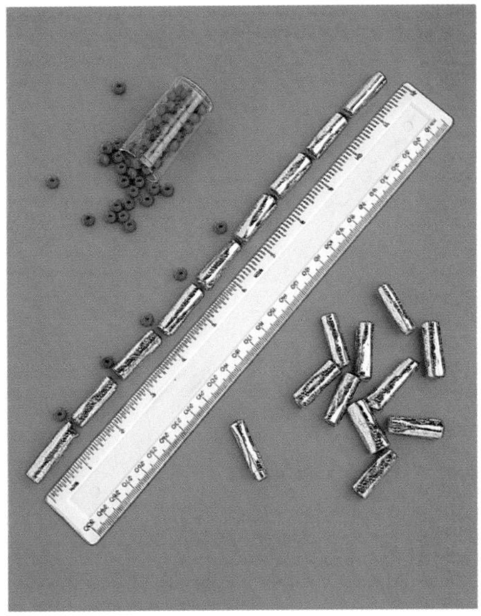

3 Rub some petroleum jelly on one end of the wooden dowel. Cover the wrong (plain) side of the paper with plenty of glue.

4 Place the dowel right at one end of the glued paper. Roll the paper around the dowel, as tightly as possible. Keep rolling up the paper to make a tube-shaped bead. Take out the dowel. Put the bead aside to dry.

5 If you are happy with the size and shape of your bead, figure out how many you will need to complete your necklace. Cut enough strips of paper to make all the beads, and roll them up as in step 4.

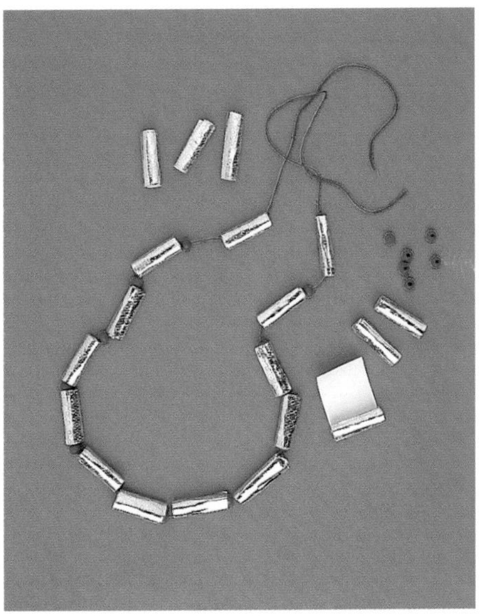

6 With the darning needle, thread the beads onto the embroidery floss. You can use bought beads to add to the necklace if you wish. When all the beads are threaded, tie the ends of the floss together neatly.

NOW TRY THIS

- **Instead of using long rectangles of paper, try making beads from long triangles. Experiment with different lengths and widths to make a variety of shapes.**
- **Make beads out of plain paper, and paint them after they have been made. When the paint is dry, "varnish" them with a coat of glue.**

FRIENDSHIP BRACELET

YOU WILL NEED

- Yarn (or cotton crochet yarn) in a variety of colors
- Stiff cardboard, about 8 x 6 in. (20 x 15 cm)
- Two pieces stiff cardboard, about 6 x 1 in. (15 x 3 cm)
- Large, blunt darning needle
- Tape
- Pencil & ruler
- Scissors

Make a colorful band and give it to a good friend. These bands are usually made from knotted thread or string, but here is another way to make them and learn about weaving at the same time.

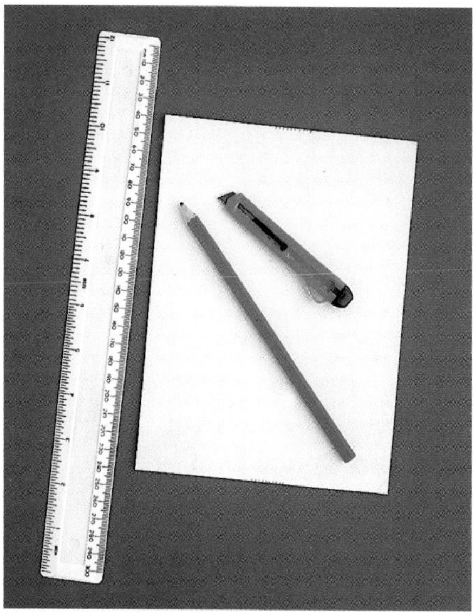

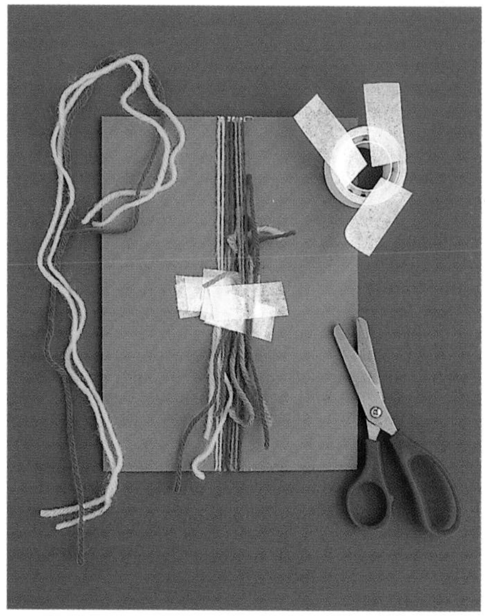

1 Take the large piece of cardboard. At each short end, in the middle, make ten small cuts, very close together. Make sure the cuts are exactly opposite each other.

2 Cut ten lengths of yarn in different colors, about 16 in. (40 cm) long. Stretch them between the notches in the cardboard, and fix them tightly in position at the back, with tape.

Some ways of weaving fabric are very simple. All that is needed is to stretch out the long threads to weave across. This African man is weaving outdoors. He has stretched his threads between some small trees.

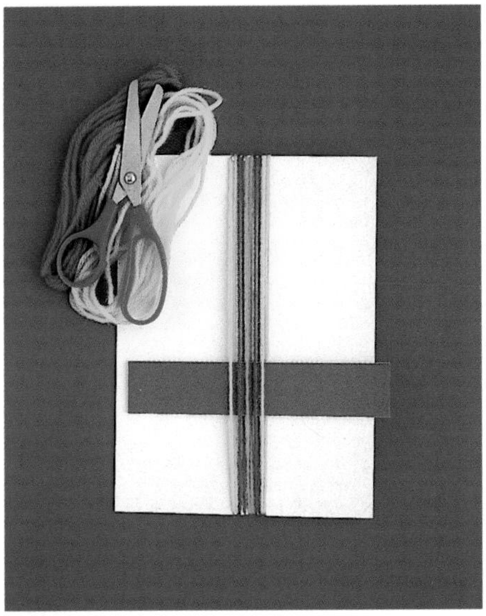

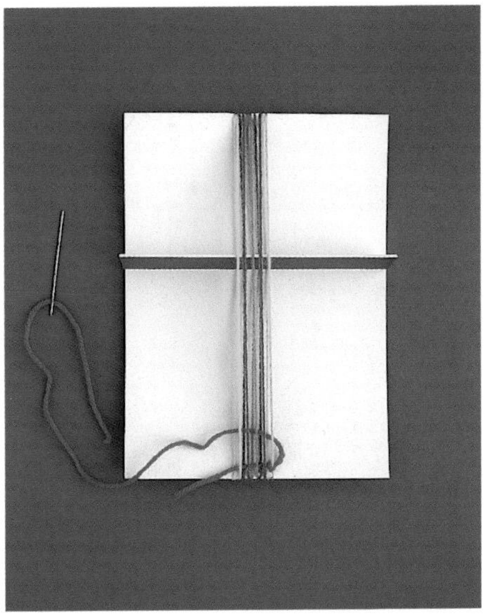

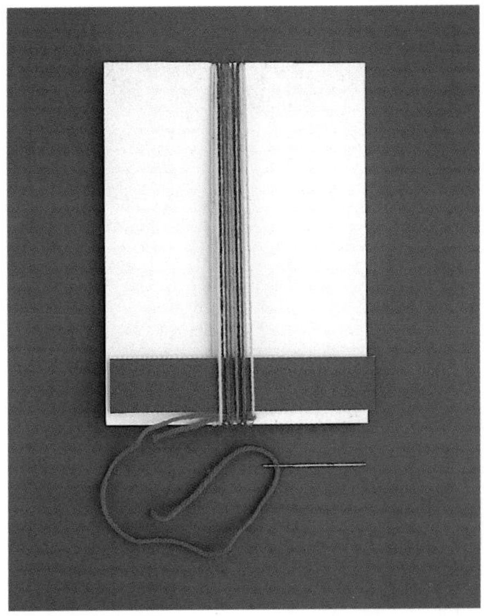

3 Take one of the strips of cardboard. Pass it under the first length of yarn, over the second, under the third, over the fourth, etc., until you reach the other side.

4 Cut a long length of yarn. Thread one end through the needle. Tie the other end to a strand of yarn at the bottom. Turn the cardboard strip so that it stands up on its side. Run the threaded needle through from one side to the other.

5 Pull the yarn tight. Then turn the cardboard strip so it is flat again, and use it to push the weaving down to the bottom. Push the cardboard strip back up and leave it where it is.

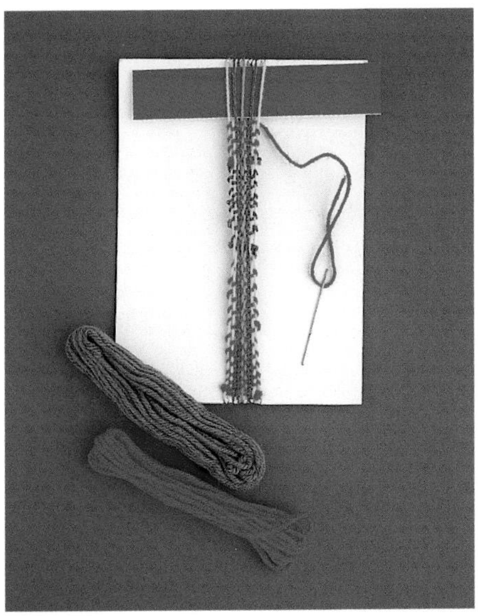

6 Using the needle, weave it through the yarn so that it goes <u>over</u> the first length of yarn, <u>under</u> the second, <u>over</u> the third, etc., until you reach the other side. Pull the needle through and use the cardboard to push the weaving down.

7 Continue until you are about 2 in. (5 cm) from the top of the cardboard. Remove the yarn from the cardboard, knot the ends so they will not come undone, and your band is ready to tie around your wrist.

BADGE WITH LIGHTS

YOU WILL NEED

- Piece of thick, lightweight cardboard, such as Styrofoam
- One or two 2-volt flashing LEDs, .25 in. (5 mm) in diameter
- Battery (4.5V minimum)
- Single-core electric wire, about 4 ft. (1.2 m)
- Wire cutter and stripper
- Large safety pin
- Masking tape
- Hole punch, same diameter as LED
- Pencil
- Hobby knife and steel ruler
- Scissors

Here is a way of using a small electrical current and flashing lights to make a badge that is unusual and fun. The lights, called LEDs, are joined with wire to a battery. Pin the badge to your clothes, with the battery hidden inside your clothing or in a pocket.

Design it to look like anything you like, such as a scary face, a spider, an animal, or even a truck with headlights.

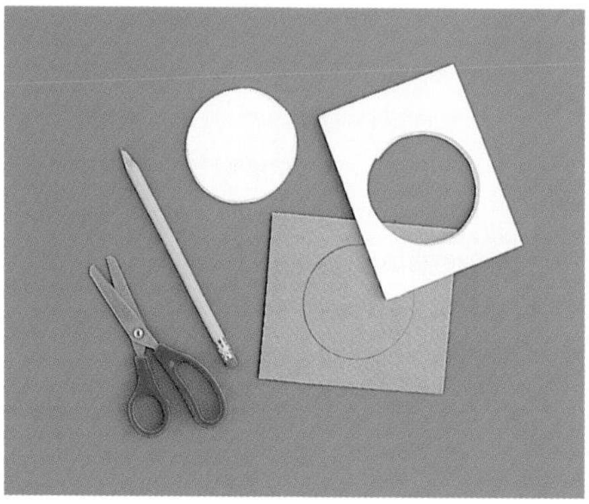

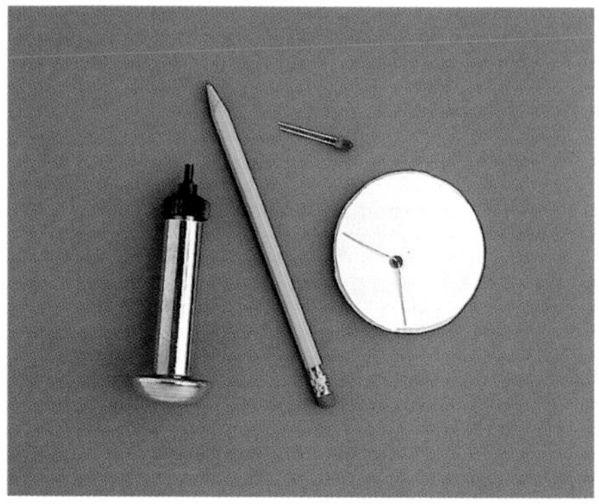

1 Draw the shape of the badge on the cardboard. Cut it out with scissors or get an adult to help you with a hobby knife.

2 Mark where the LED is to go. Punch a hole in the cardboard. Push the LED through the hole and flatten its wire legs onto the cardboard.

A badge usually tells us something about the person who is wearing it. It may give the person's name or show that he or she belongs to a club. Sometimes a badge shows someone's job or age. Other badges have messages on them or just bright pictures.

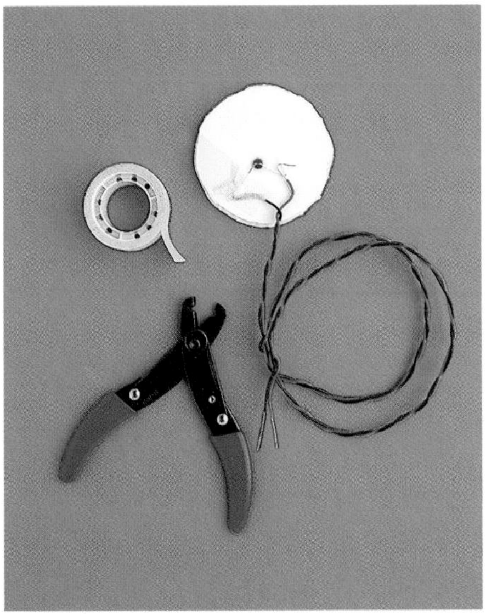

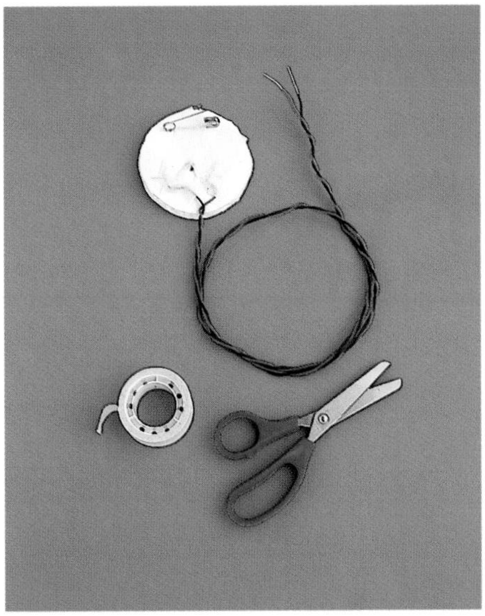

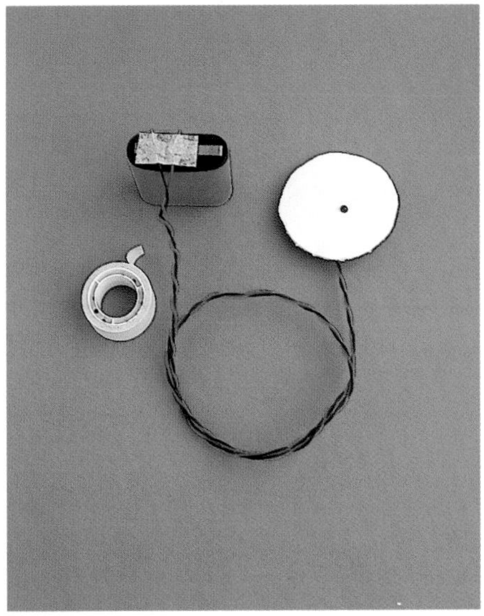

3 Cut two lengths of wire about 2 ft. (60 cm) long. Strip about .75 in. (2 cm) of the plastic covering from each end of the wires. Join an end to each leg of the LED. Twist the wires together all the way down their length.

4 Stick the safety pin to the back of the badge with several pieces of masking tape. Make sure the pin side is facing outward.

5 You will have to attach the other end of each wire to a battery terminal. Use masking tape to keep the wires in place. If the LED does not work, switch the ends over to the opposite terminals.

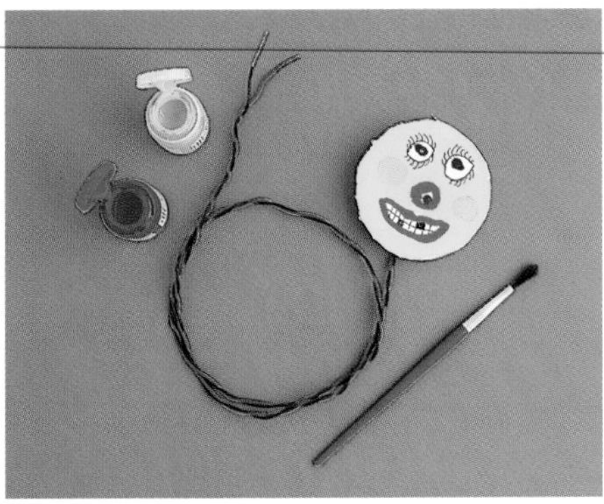

6 Decorate the badge, making sure that the LED is part of your design. When the paint is dry, pin the badge to your shirt, and put the battery inside your shirt or in a shirt pocket.

A hobby knife can be dangerous if it is not used properly. Always ask an adult to help you use one.

- **To avoid accidents, never play with sharp knives.**
- **Use a steel ruler to guide the knife.**

CLOAK

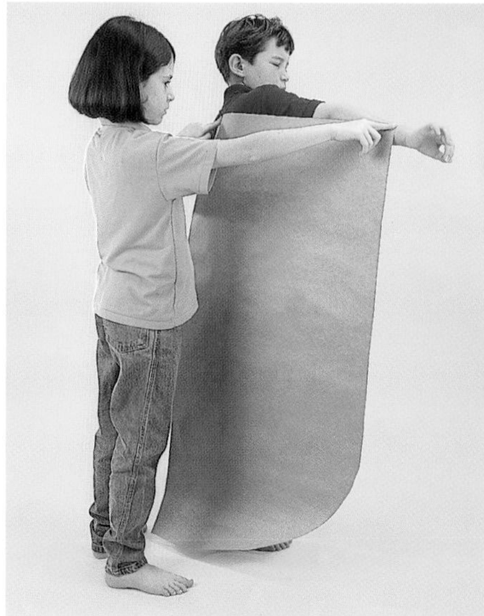

1 Measure the person who is going to wear the cloak. Find the length from the back of the neck, to just above the floor.

2 With the person's arms outstretched, measure the width from one wrist, across the back, to the other wrist.

3 Make a paper pattern for the cloak. It should be the same length as step 1 and half the width measured in step 2. Make the bottom curved at one corner. Cut out the pattern. Hold it up against the person to make sure it is the correct size.

YOU WILL NEED

- Fabric (see steps 1 and 2 for measurements)
- Five adhesive Velcro pieces
- Large sheet of paper, such as brown paper
- Long-sleeved shirt
- Tape measure
- Pencil
- Scissors

Many years ago, cloaks were often worn instead of overcoats. A cloak can be fun to wear as it swirls around or floats behind the person wearing it.

To make this cloak, it is important to measure the person who will be wearing it. It is joined to his or her shirt with Velcro fasteners.

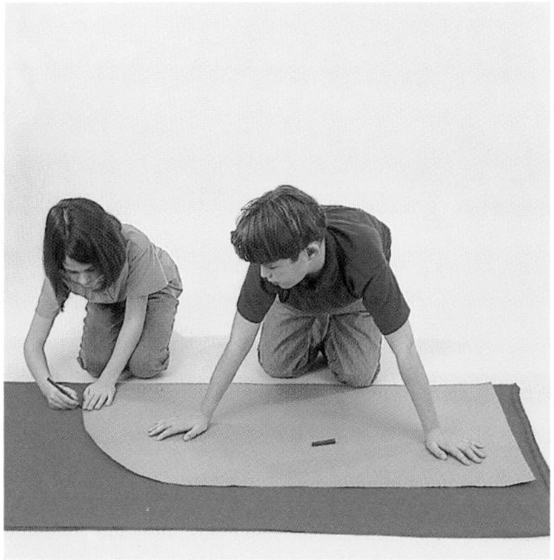

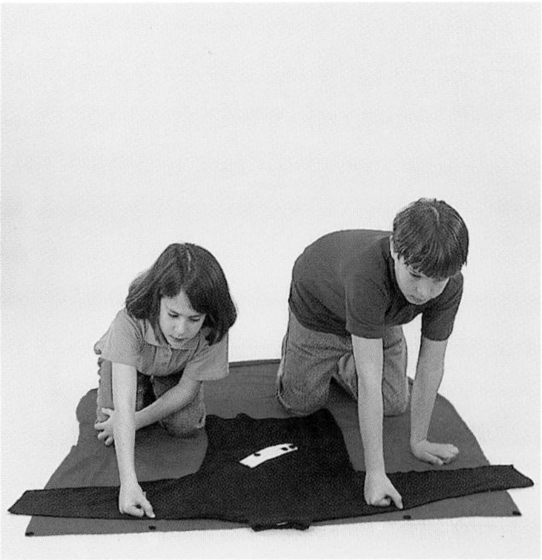

4 Fold the fabric in half and lay it out flat on the floor. Put the paper pattern on top of it. Make sure the long, center edge is right against the fold. Draw around the edges with pencil or felt-tip pen. Cut out the fabric.

5 Open out the fabric and lay it flat, wrong side out. Stick Velcro pieces along the top edge. Space them evenly. Make sure they are on the wrong side of the fabric.

6 Put the other halves of the fastener dots along the arms and neck of a long-sleeved shirt. They should be the same distance apart as on the cloak.

7 Put on the long-sleeved shirt. Press the two rows of dots together—and the cloak is finished.

This cloak is worn by a Native American. It shows a crow made of red fabric decorated with buttons.

NOW TRY THIS

Once you have seen how this cloak is made, design another with a more complex shape. It could have pleats at the top or a jagged lower edge, like a bat's wings.

CARNIVAL COSTUME

Carnivals are like big parties and are usually held outdoors. In the famous carnivals, such as the one in Rio de Janeiro, Brazil, people dress in fantastic costumes that can take many months to make.

Use your imagination to design your own costume made out of recycled materials. It could be anything from an animal to a rocket, or a robot to a skeleton. Draw a picture of how you would like your costume to look.

YOU WILL NEED

- Cardboard boxes
- Fabric tape, about 2 in. (5 cm) wide and 24 in. (60 cm) long
- Large metal paper fasteners
- Cardboard (for head piece, optional)
- Various papers such as brown, crepe, tissue, and newspaper
- Paints and brushes (optional)
- Masking tape
- Glue
- Scissors
- Pencil
- Plain paper for drawing

1 Find a cardboard box that will go around the top part of your body. Cut off, or fold out, the top and the bottom, and try it on to make sure it fits around you.

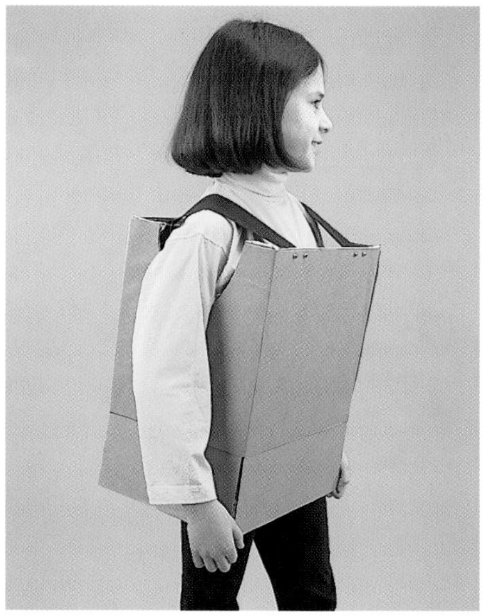

2 Hang the box from your shoulders, using wide fabric tape, attached at either end with the large metal paper fasteners. Cut holes on both sides for your arms.

Some carnival costumes have big frames that are decorated with different materials in bright colors. The costumes are supported on people's shoulders. The wearers have to keep the costumes on as they dance around the streets.

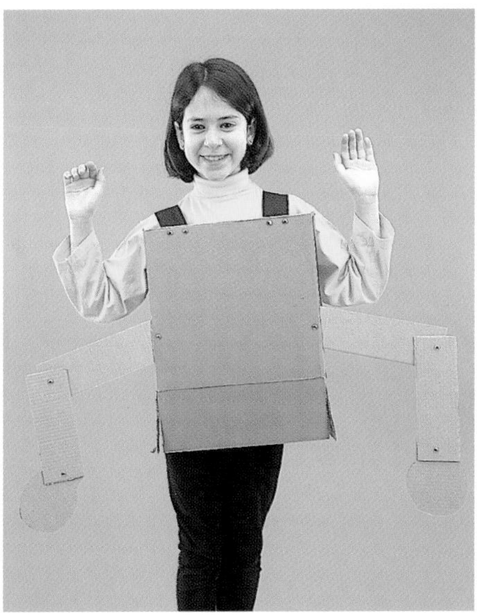

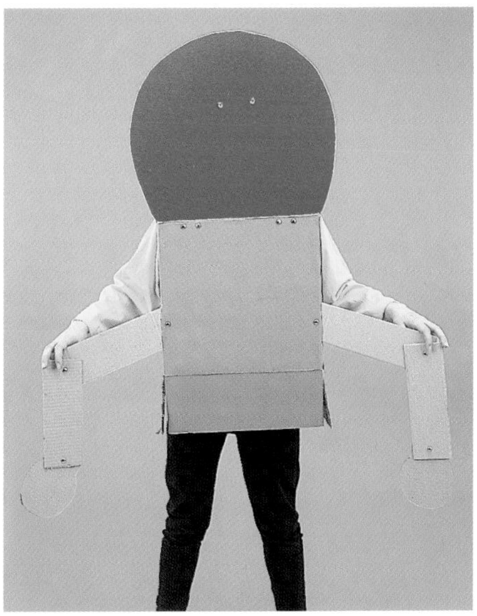

3 Add extra shapes to the box. You can make them in different ways. For example, cut them out of cardboard from old boxes. Make joints that move, using metal paper fasteners. Or use paper or fabric joined with masking tape.

4 Put a headpiece on the costume. It can be taller than the top of your head. Use masking tape to join some cardboard to the box to hold up the shape. Remember to make eye holes so that you can see.

5 Decorate the entire costume by using colored paper or by painting the paper and cardboard. Don't forget to make your legs and arms part of the costume. Let the paint and any glue dry before wearing it.

GLOSSARY

brim The edge of a hat that sticks out.

ceremony A way of doing things on a special occasion, such as when people get married, or when dead people are buried.

crease A line or wrinkle made by folding. Creases can be made in paper, cardboard, and fabric.

diameter The distance across the center of a circle, from one side to the other.

disk A flat, circular shape.

fabric Material that has been woven or knitted, using thread or yarn, for example.

fake Something that is not what it is supposed to be; not genuine or real.

frame A strong shape that can hold up things stuck to it.

gem A precious stone that has been cut and polished, such as a diamond, emerald, or ruby.

hinge A joint that moves, letting things, such as a door, swing open or shut.

jewelry Gems or ornaments worn on a person's body.

LED Short for Light-Emitting Diode. An LED is like a tiny light bulb.

lens A piece of glass or plastic that is curved on one or both sides. The curve bends rays of light.

mirror image The exact reverse of a shape, as though it has been reflected in a mirror.

pattern Pieces of paper that show how to cut out fabric for clothes; also decoration on paper or fabric.

pleat A flat double fold in a piece of cloth.

rectangle A shape with four sides, where two opposite sides of the same length are longer than the other two sides.

terminal The parts of a battery where other things—such as wires—can be joined to it.

traditional Something that has been done or used for hundreds of years is traditional.

weaving Making flat fabric by lacing together long threads running in two directions.

wrong side The side of paper, cardboard, or fabric that does not have the color or a pattern on it.

BOOKS TO READ

Badt, Karin L. *On Your Feet*. World of Difference. Danbury, CT: Children's Press, 1994.

Casey, Kevin K. *Costumes*. Customs, Costumes, and Cultures. Vero Beach, FL: Rourke Publishing Group, 1996.

Earl, Amanda and Danielle Sensier. *Masks*. Traditions Around the World. New York: Thomson Learning, 1995.

Jackson, Mike. *Clothes From Many Lands*. Read All About It. Austin, TX: Raintree Steck-Vaughn, 1995.

Rowland-Warne, L. *Costume*. Eyewitness Books. New York: Knopf Books for Young Readers, 1992.

Tythacott, Louise. *Jewelry*. Traditions Around the World. New York: Thomson Learning, 1995.

Westray, Kathleen. *Clothes From Head to Toe*. New York: Ticknor and Fields, 1995.

ADDITIONAL NOTES

Royal Crown While children should be allowed as much freedom as possible to make designs, they can also be encouraged to research and examine "real" examples. This project provides excellent opportunities to link with cross-curricular topics in drama and history.

Bow Tie This method allows children to create an item out of fabric, but without a stitch of sewing. A crisp cotton that creases easily under pressure from the fingertips is ideal. To avoid distortion when creasing, the fabric must be cut on the straight grain (i.e., parallel to the direction of the fibers). It is a good opportunity to examine the "right" and "wrong" sides of printed fabric and could lead to craft-linked exercises in simple printing techniques.

Barrettes Materials for decoration must be chosen carefully to ensure that they will adhere to the masking tape surface, using just glue. Durability is addressed in step 5, and children could experiment with different materials, evaluating performance over time.

Make Your Own Hat Measuring the head and getting the hat to fit is of paramount importance for a successful result. Although somewhat similar to the crown project, the method of construction requires greater precision and skill. Once children have grasped the basic principles, they should be encouraged to experiment with a variety of different shapes.

Eyeglasses An ideal opportunity to explain symmetry. Some confusion may arise at first between one shape being symmetrical and two shapes being mirror images of each other.

Sandals Tracing around and comparing foot shapes will help children understand the need for different sizes of footwear. The band across the foot is covered in self-adhesive vinyl for reinforcement. It may be useful to guide children through experimentation with various materials for this band, to open the way for discussion on both comfort and durability.

Face Mask Another opportunity to link technology with cross-curricular topics such as geography and other cultures. It may be helpful to use tape to cover the legs of the paper fasteners, once joined, to avoid scratches on children's faces.

Necklace Measurement is an essential part of this project, both in establishing the finished length of the necklace and by dividing this by the width of the beads to calculate the number needed.

Friendship Bracelet This teaches the basic principles of weaving to produce a result that children will find appealing. Some children may need help to thread the needle, by twisting the yarn into a tight spiral loop before pushing it firmly into the needle's eye.

Badge with Lights This uses a simple electrical circuit to enliven a straightforward project. Flashing LEDs are available from electronic suppliers in a variety of colors. The correct connection to the battery is easily found by experimentation.

Cloak Measuring is the most important facet of this project. Take care to use the correct variety of Velcro fasteners: those that are sufficiently sticky and do not require sewing in place. Lightweight fabric is also advisable.

Carnival Costume An opportunity for children to indulge creative talents to the full, building on the basic structure explained in the steps, using a variety of materials in an imaginative way.

INDEX

Acknowledgments

The author and publishers wish to thank the following for their kind assistance with this book: models Josie Kearns, Yasmin Mukhida, Charlotte Page, Tom Rigby, and Ranga Silva. Also Gabriella Casemore, Zul Mukhida, Philippa Smith, and Gus Ferguson.

For the use of their library photographs, grateful thanks are due to Bryan and Cherry Alexander p5 (bottom); Eye Ubiquitous p11 (Frank Leather), p20 (Matthew McKee), p28–29 (David Cumming); James Davis Travel Photography, p4, p19; Popperfoto/John Stillwell p7; Zul/Chapel Studios p5 top (Graham Horner), p15, p27.
All other photographs belong to the Wayland Picture Library: p12, p17 (Jimmy Holmes), p22, p24.